BRIDGES
OF THE WORLD

BRIDGES
OF THE WORLD

FROM ANTIQUITY THROUGH
TO TODAY'S SUPERSTRUCTURES

DAVID ROSS

amber
BOOKS

Published by
Amber Books Ltd
United House
North Road
London
N7 9DP
United Kingdom
www.amberbooks.co.uk
Appstore: itunes.com/apps/amberbooksltd
Facebook: www.facebook.com/amberbooks
Twitter: @amberbooks

Project Editor: Sarah Uttridge
Designers: Keren Harragan and Andrew Easton
Picture Research: Terry Forshaw

ISBN: 978-1-78274-626-3

Printed in China

1 4 6 8 10 9 7 5 3 2

Contents

Introduction 6

Ancient and Medieval Bridges 62BCE–1499 8

Early Modern Bridges 1500–1700 48

18th & 19th Century Bridges 84

20th Century Bridges 126

21st Century Bridges 178

Picture Credits 224

Introduction

The first bridges were perhaps no more than tree-trunks conveniently fallen between river banks, but it is likely that simple bridges were among the earliest human constructions. Flat stone slabs resting on river-bed rocks or piled stones – known as 'clapper bridges' in England – may have prehistoric origins. These were suitable only for shallow streams. A momentous advance came when the principle of the arch was worked out and put into effect, enabling wider spans and a degree of freedom from spates and floods. Ever since these ancient times, the concept of the bridge as a joining agency has had a powerful effect on people's imagination. Bridges as symbols are always positive, conveying a sense of balance, discovery and peaceful progress. We talk about 'building bridges' to eliminate misunderstandings and hostility, and the modern fad of attaching padlocks to certain bridges is an application of the same idea.

The bridges in this book have played and continue to play a vital part in social and economic life across the continents. Viewing them gives a real and many-layered feeling of satisfaction, its roots as deep as human history.

ABOVE:
Ponte Di Rialto, Venice, Italy
RIGHT:
Dongting Lake Bridge, Yueyang, China

Ancient and Medieval Bridges
62 BCE–1499

The origins of arched construction, in which shaped stones are fitted together and held up by the pressure of the blocks upon one another, have been traced back into the prehistory of the Middle East, though no arched bridges survive from this remote period. The Greeks made limited use of arches, but the great development of the principle was made by the Romans. In Rome, arched structures survive from around the 5th century BCE as drain coverings. By the first century BCE, Roman engineers were spanning rivers and gorges with arched bridges. Their arches were always semicircular, which meant that the width of each span was limited by the height of the bridge.

Roman bridges followed the spread of Roman roads and Roman settlements, many of which required aqueducts to provide a regular water supply. Hundreds of these bridges and aqueducts survived in use for centuries after the collapse of the Roman Empire, and were renewed or replaced by bridges on the same sites and built in very much the same fashion. New techniques were adopted gradually, often beginning outside Europe, in the new Islamic states and in imperial China. Introduction of pointed arches, and of up-curving or apexed bridge decks, allowing for greater height and so wider spans, led to some remarkable bridges from around the 9th century onwards. By the end of the medieval period, a variety of bridge types had emerged. In towns, bridges often became sites for markets and shops, and also for houses.

LEFT:
Kapellbrücke (Chapel Bridge), Lucerne, Switzerland
Wood was probably the material of the very first bridges and is still often used. This is the oldest surviving roofed bridge in Europe, built between 1333 and 1365. Crossing the River Reuss, until 1835 it was 278m (912ft) long, but filling in of the bank has reduced it to 202.9m (666ft). It was restored after a fire in 1993.

Ponte Fabricio, Rome, Italy
The oldest bridge in Rome
still to be largely in its original
state, it links the Campus
Martius to the Tiber Island.
Commissioned by and named
for Lucius Fabricius, Curator
of Roads, and built in 62 BCE
of volcanic stone known as
peperino, it is 62m (203ft)
long and 5.5m (18ft) wide.
The original marble facing was
replaced by bricks in 1679.

Puente Trajan (Trajan's Bridge), Alcántara, Estremadura, Spain
Commissioned by Emperor Trajan in 98 CE, designed by Caius Julius Lacer, and built over the Tagus without mortar in 104–06 CE, with six arches, the total length is 181.7m (596ft), width 8.6m (28.2ft), and height 45m (147.6ft). A triumphal arch above the central pier is inscribed: "I have built a bridge which will last for ever."

ABOVE:

Ponte di Tiberio (Tiberius Bridge), Rimini, Italy
Named for Emperor Tiberius, it was completed between 14 and 21 CE, with five arches formed of Istrian marble, carrying the Via Aemilia over the Marecchia River (now a canal). Its length is 62.6m (205.3ft), and its width of 8.6m (28ft) was determined by the breadth of an army column.

RIGHT:

Acueducto de los Milagros (Aqueduct of the Miracles), Mérida, Spain
Carrying water to the Roman city of Emerita Augusta, over the Albarregas River, this aqueduct was built soon after 100 CE, when Roman engineering reached a high point during the reign of Trajan. Nowadays, it is favoured by storks for nest-building. Its maximum height is 30m (98.5ft) and the longest span between piers is 4.5m (14.8ft).

Pont du Gard, Nîmes, France
Built over the Gard River between 40 and 60 CE, 275m (902ft) long, it is the highest Roman aqueduct (50m, 164 ft), once carrying around 200,000 cubic metres of water a day, on an imperceptible gradient of 1/3000. Its two lower levels were built without mortar. In use as an aqueduct until the 6th century, it owed its survival to being used as a roadway.

Puente Romano (Roman Bridge), Córdoba, Spain
Stretching for 250m (820ft) over the Guadalquivir River, the bridge carried the Via Augusta and dates from the early 1st century CE. It was substantially rebuilt by Moorish rulers in the 8th century, with 16 arches rather than the original 17. The statue of St Raphael was added in the 17th century.

Segovia Aqueduct, Spain

This 119-arch aqueduct is still in use, though a concrete pipe has replaced the old Roman water channel. It was completed around 110–12 CE in 'opus quadratum', of 20,400 un-mortared granite blocks. No two of its piers are identical, suggesting that it was built by 'rule of thumb' rather than a detailed plan. Its gradient is 1.6%, length 683m (2240ft), height 29m (95ft).

Segura Aqueduct, Castelo Branco, Portugal

Spanning the River Egres on the Portuguese-Spanish border since the 2nd century CE, this five-arched waterway was rebuilt in the 16th century, retaining its variously-sized arches. Its pillars now rest on stepped bases, unseen except at low water, to minimise scour effect by the fast-moving stream.

Adana Roman Bridge, Turkey
In Turkish, Taşköprü (stone bridge), it crosses the Seyhan River with 12 spans of varying width, the longest being beneath the low apex. Dating to the first half of the 2nd century CE, it was restored in the reign of Justinian (6th century), when the river was temporarily diverted, and again under Arab rule in the 9th century.

LEFT:

Aqueduct of Aspendos, Turkey

The ruins of this 2nd century CE Roman structure preserve an inverted siphon system, formed of three 'venter' bridges, separated by two massive towers, in each of which the water rose to a higher level (still below that of the source). This enabled a cheaper, lower-level archway rather than one 55m (180ft) high, across a valley 1670m (5479ft) wide.

RIGHT:

Aqueduct of Valens, Istanbul, Turkey

Originally 925m (3034ft) long, a 625m (2050ft) stretch of this 4th century limestone aqueduct, 28m (92ft) high, still dominates the western entry to Istanbul, marking the end of a 150km (94 mile) water supply route. It replaced an earlier structure in 373 CE during the reign of Valens, was repaired in the 6th century and again in the 16th.

Malabadi Bridge, Diyarbakir Province, Turkey
Dated to 1146–47, this bridge over the Batman River marks
a new design phase with its inverted v-shape profile and
pointed arch, the widest span of its time (46.8 m, 154 ft), also
incorporating a right-angle bend in its 3-arched approach.
Interior chambers reduce weight on the foundations,
displaying the progressive approach to
engineering under the Artuqid dynasty.

OPPOSITE:

TOP LEFT:
**Anji (Zhaozhu) Bridge,
Hebei Province, China**
China's oldest surviving
bridge, built under the Sui
dynasty 581–618 CE. Its 37m
(121ft) single span is formed
from 28 limestone arches set
side by side and bonded with
iron dovetails. It is also the
oldest and perhaps the first
bridge with open spandrels,
giving it a strikingly modern
appearance. Anji translates as
'safe crossing'.

TOP RIGHT:
**Dicle Bridge, Diyarbakir,
Turkey**
On this 10-arched bridge over
the Tigris River, completed
in 1065, the architect's name,
Sancaroğlu Ubeydoğlu Yusuf,
is still visible in Kufic script
on the wall. Built of black
basalt, it is 178m (584ft) long
and 5.6m (18.3ft) wide, with a
main span of 14.7m (48ft).

BOTTOM:
**Puente la Reina (Queen's
Bridge), Navarre, Spain**
Two pilgrim routes to
Santiago converge here, and
this 110m (361ft) bridge was
built by order of Queen Doña
Mayor between 1035 and
1050 to enable them to cross
the Rio Arga. Its tall central
arch is almost pointed rather
than a traditional semicircle.
The relieving arches above the
piers are to lighten the weight,
rather than for floods.

Pont Vieux (Old Bridge), Albi, France
Completed in 1040, it is 150m (492ft) long, with a main span of 21.4m (70ft). It was a toll bridge (as almost all large bridges were) on the trade route across southern France, with fortified gates at each end, and a central chapel. Seven houses were built on it between the 14th century and 1766.

LEFT:

High Bridge, Lincoln, England

The oldest bridge in Great Britain still carrying houses, its ribbed arch was built across the River Witham around 1160. Originally used as a fish market, half-timbered houses were built on it from 1540. A restoration was done in 1902, when storage rooms within the northern part of the bridge structure were sealed up.

OPPOSITE, TOP & BOTTOM:

Lugou or Marco Polo Bridge, Beijing, China

Crossing the Yangdong River, the granite bridge was still new (built 1189–92) when the Italian traveller Marco Polo described it. A reconstruction was done in 1698. With 11 spans, it is 266.5m (874ft) long. The walkway is lined by 281 pillars featuring stone lions, added at various times between 1192 and 1644.

Vieux Pont (Old Bridge), Béziers, France

On the *route royale* from Paris to Perpignan, with 10 main arches bridging the River Orb, the 260m (853ft) long structure dates from the 12th century. Alterations were made in succeeding centuries, notably the 1840s, before its restoration to something like its pre-1840 condition in the 1960s.

Hasankeyf Bridge, Anatolia, Turkey
Like the Malabadi Bridge, this was an engineering triumph
of the Artuqid period, built 1147–72. Originally four-arched,
with a very large central span, it collapsed or was destroyed by
the mid-17th century. Its remains are likely to disappear by the
2020s with the construction of the Ilisu dam on the Tigris.

Salahin Bridge, Alaverdi, Armenia
A late 12th century bridge over the Debed River, said to have been built for the funeral of King Abas Kyvrikyan, and constructed from basalt blocks. Its roadway is stepped, and the parapets have high-relief lion carvings on the apex. It is 60m (197ft) long, with a main span of 18.6m (61ft).

LEFT:

Citadel Bridge, Aleppo, Syria

The ancient citadel of Aleppo was greatly enlarged in 1193–1215 by Sultan al-Zahir al Ghazi, with this fortified bridge rising over the moat as the only access. Its massive piers and narrow arches were intended to make it indestructible. Though damaged in the 21st century civil war, it still stands.

RIGHT:

Ponts Couverts, Strasbourg, France

In a 13th-century extension of the city boundary, the three 'Covered Bridges' and four towers, over the Ill River, formed part of the defensive wall. The wooden roofs of the bridges were removed in 1784, almost a century after they had been superseded by new defences, but the name remained.

OPPOSITE LEFT AND LEFT:
Monnow Bridge, Monmouth, Wales
The only surviving fortified bridge in Britain with a tower on the bridge itself, it was built around 1200–1210 of red sandstone to replace a wooden predecessor. The gatehouse, dating from 1297–1315, was rebuilt with side arches after 1705, by which time it was a toll-booth rather than a defence.

BELOW:
Starý Most (Old Bridge), Písek, South Bohemia, Czech Republic
Claimed to be the oldest stone bridge in the Czech Republic, and second-oldest in Central Europe, it was built over the Otava River between 1250 and 1275. Partially destroyed by a flood in 2002, it was rebuilt in a discreetly strengthened form. The statues of saints which line it are replicas, the surviving originals now housed in a museum.

ABOVE:

Ponte Castelvecchio, Verona, Italy
At low water, Roman stonework can be seen at the bases of this fortified bridge over the Adige River, linking the castle to the city. Built in 1354–57, 102m (334.6ft) long, of red and white marble and terracotta bricks, with typical Ghibelline 'swallowtail' battlements, and a massive tower at each end, it is a high point of 14th-century military architecture.

RIGHT:

Kraemerbrücke (Merchant's Bridge), Erfurt, Germany
Bridging the Breitstrom arm of the River Gera, it is the largest still-inhabited bridge in the world. Built in 1325, it originally held market stalls, but, after rebuilding in 1472, 62 houses were built out on trusses, in two rows. Restoration work was carried out between 1969 and 1973.

Pont Valentré, Cahors, France
Three towers guard this bridge across the River Lot, with six main arches and sharp-angled piers rising to parapet level. The order to build was given in 1306, the crossing completed by 1345 and the towers in place by around 1380. A restoration was made in 1880, incorporating a devil sculpture on the central tower to denote the bridge's nickname of '*pont du diable*'.

Puente de San Martin, Toledo, Spain
Spanning the Tagus River with five pointed arches and a fortified tower at each end, its 27m (88.6ft) height between high banks enabled a level profile despite a main span of 40m (131ft). It was completed in 1380, using squared granite blocks, was partially rebuilt in 1690 and repaved in 1710. It has been a national historical monument since 1921.

Puente de Frías, Burgos Province, Spain
A fortified bridge, 143m (469ft) long, it carries the old trading route to the north coast over the Ebro River. It was probably completed in the years after 1214, with the pentagonal tower added in the 14th century. Much evidence of repair and later buttressing can be seen. Its 3.4m (11ft) width shows it was intended for horse and donkey traffic only.

Ponte Vecchio (Old Bridge), Florence, Italy
The really striking thing about this bridge is the shape of its
arches, neither semi circular nor pointed, with a maximum
span of 30m (98.4ft), designed to span the Arno River with the
minimum of support. Generally regarded as the first segmental-
arched bridge to be built in Western Europe, it is certainly the
oldest, completed in 1345. Its two-storey gallery has always
been devoted to commerce, reserved to jewellers and goldsmiths
since 1593.

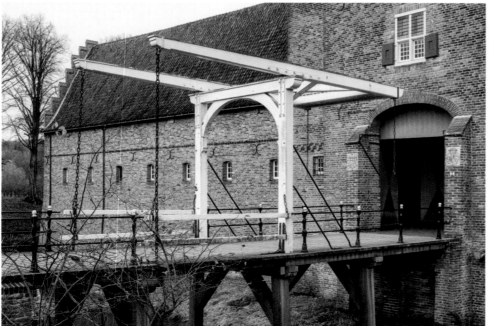

TOP LEFT:

Ponte Visconti, Valeggio sul Mincio, Italy
Part bridge, part-dam, built in 1393, it is a key element in a complex system of fortifications and river deviations. Made of laterite stone, and locally known as the 'long bridge', it was partially destroyed in 1701 (the metal span was inserted in the 1920s), but its arches and towers still dominate the landscape.

BOTTOM LEFT:

Kasteel Doorwerth, Gelderland, Netherlands
The castle of Doorwerth is a moated 15th-century building, entered over a drawbridge. Originally the winding gear would have been within the walls, but the present bridge is external, a typical Dutch bascule type developed from the 1600s or earlier. Weights attached to the pivoted upper booms counterbalance the weight of the bridge, making it easy to raise and lower it with the use of windlasses.

ABOVE:

Obere Brücke (Upper Bridge), Bamberg, Germany
Spanning an arm of the Regnitz River, its arches separated by a small island, the bridge replaced an older structure in 1455. The building is the rococo and half-timbered style *Altes Rathaus* or old Town Hall, built between 1744 and 1756, with a through passage for pedestrians. The central arch, of three, was destroyed in 1945 and rebuilt in 1956.

Karlův Most (Charles Bridge), Prague, Czech Republic
Named for Emperor Charles IV, before 1870 it was simply 'the Stone Bridge'. Built over the Vltava River between 1357 and 1402, of Bohemian sandstone, it has a fortified tower at each end. Its 16 arches vary in span, from 16.62 to 23.28m (54.5 to 84ft. The thirty statues which line it are now replicas of the originals.

Early Modern Bridges 1500–1700

Some of the most important changes in bridge design during these two centuries are not easily seen. One of them was the steady widening of the roadways. Roman bridges had been built with an eye to a marching military column, or the passage of a single despatch rider, and medieval bridges were hardly wider. Now builders in cities and towns, and wealthier country districts, had to think in terms of carriages and wagons, and also of guns and siege machinery, and so build, or rebuild, bridges wide and strong enough to bear heavy axle-loads. It was a very gradual process and many bridges were still built to narrow dimensions and with a humpback shape that made haulage difficult. Along with widening went strengthening: the wider arches were more vulnerable to sagging or collapse. This compelled builders to think hard and creatively about constructional problems and gain a better understanding of the forces a bridge must withstand. There was another consequence too: bridges became more expensive, requiring better materials, stronger foundations, and greater skill from the masons; but this was not a serious problem when trade was expanding and the beginnings of industry, though still powered by wind and water, were evident.

LEFT:
Brig o' Doon, Alloway, Scotland
Like all older bridges, this 16th-century bridge across the River Doon (first mentioned in 1512) has been often repaired while still retaining its essential structure and character. An archivolt of dressed stone lines the arch on each side and the roadway is formed of cobble-stones. It is celebrated in Robert Burns's poem 'Tam o' Shanter'.

Slaters' Bridge, Cumbria, England
Built in the late 18th century across the River Brathay, this combination of arch and slab was on a pack-horse route to carry slates from quarries in the hills. The voussoirs (arch stones) are up to 1.3m (4.3ft) long. The width of only 1.27m (4.2ft) required very careful passage.

Old Bridge, Stirling, Scotland

For centuries the only crossing of the River Forth was here. This 16th-century bridge of four unribbed semicircular arches had wooden predecessors. The ashlar (cut stone) spans are all of different widths, the widest being 17m (55.8ft), but in the same style, with decorative mouldings. Stone pylons at each end denote the importance of the bridge.

ABOVE:
Dyavolski Most (Devil's Bridge), Ardino, Bulgaria
One of numerous bridges still showing the skill of Ottoman
builders. Built between 1515 and 1518, set directly on bedrock,
it carries the old Roman Via Ignacia, which ran from the
Aegean coast to northern Thrace, over the River Arda. Its main
span is 56.4m (185ft) and the apex is 11.5m (37.7ft) above the
stream. Its name comes from a legendary pact between its
builder, Dimitar, and the Devil.

RIGHT:
Bar Aqueduct, Stari Bar, Montenegro
Once the final section of a water supply system, completed
around the end of the 16th century, its 17 arches are built of
rough-cut stone and originally carried stoneware pipes within a
covered top deck. It has been rebuilt twice, once after a siege in
1877 and more completely following a devastating earthquake
in April 1979.

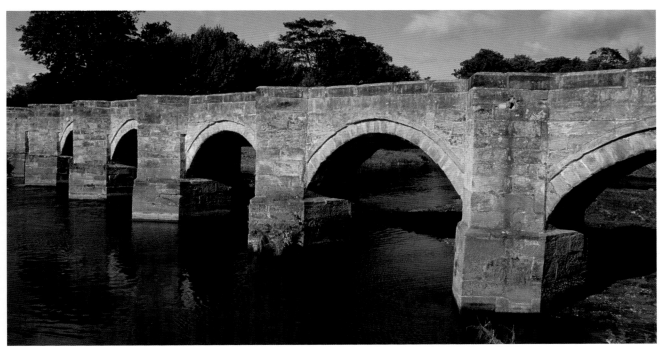

ABOVE AND RIGHT:

Essex Bridge, Shugborough, England
Packhorse bridges were narrow, with low parapets to allow
loaded horses to cross. At 100m (328ft) this is the longest
surviving example, built during the 17th century, spanning the
River Trent. Passing places were made above the piers, using
their protruding cutwaters. Maximum width is 2m (6.6ft).

LEFT:

Stari Most ('Old Bridge'), Mostar, Bosnia-Herzegovina
A masterpiece of Ottoman architecture, designed by Mimar
Hayruddin, it spanned the Neretva River from 1566 until
destroyed by gunfire in 1993. It was rebuilt and reopened in
2004. Of limestone masonry, its span is 27m (88.6ft), and
its width 4m (13.1ft). From its apex, local youths dive 24m
(78.7ft) into the river.

Padre Tembleque Aqueduct, Tepeyahualco, Mexico
Part of a vast hydraulic irrigation system, the initiative of
Franciscan friars, this striking aqueduct was built between
1555 and 1572. Its 68 arches cross the Tepeyahualco Ravine
and Papalote River, with a maximum height of 33.84m (111ft).
The brickwork construction combined European technology
and Mesoamerican building techniques, using adobe formwork
rather than scaffolding.

ABOVE:

Mehmed Paša Sokolović Bridge, Visegrad, Bosnia-Herzegovina
Designed by the great architect Mimar Sinan, completed in 1577, this classic Ottoman viaduct crosses the Drina River on 11 ashlar limestone spans, varying from 11 to 15m (36–53.8ft) and with a total length of 179.5m (589ft). On the left bank a four-arched access ramp meets the main structure at right angles.

RIGHT:

Ponte dei Tre Archi, Venice, Italy
Venice's only triple-arched bridge, it was named Ponte di San Giobbe when built over the Cannaregio Canal in 1688. It was modified in a 1794 rebuild, but retained its distinctive profile and design, red brick contrasting with white Istrian limestone. The steps are paved with volcanic trachite.

Puente de Segovia, Madrid, Spain

Madrid's oldest bridge, over the Manzanares River, completed in 1584. Pointed granite cutwaters protect the northern piers of its nine semicircular arches, with rounded ones on the south side. Granite spheres decorate the parapets. Destroyed during the Spanish Civil War, it was rebuilt by 1960, 31m (101.7ft) wide rather than the original 8.5m (27.9ft), though its outward appearance was preserved.

RIGHT:

Seher-Ćehajina Ćuprija (Governor's Bridge), Sarajevo, Bosnia-Herzegovina

Floods on the Miljacka River have had their effect on this limestone bridge. Originally five-arched, now four, it was built by the city governor's order in 1585–86. Partially washed away on at least four occasions, it has always been rebuilt. In 1904, its stone parapets were replaced by externally mounted iron-railed pavements, and restored in 1998.

LEFT:

Japanese Covered Bridge, Hoi An, Vietnam
The local Japanese community built this 19.8m (65ft) bridge between 1593 and 1595, called in Vietnamese 'Lai Vien Kieu' (bridge for passengers from afar). It is wholly Japanese in style, with a small temple in the centre. Figures of a dog and a monkey perhaps represent the years of start and inauguration. Its original hump form, flattened for the convenience of motorists, was restored in 1986.

RIGHT:

Ponte di Rialto, Venice, Italy
The first bridging point of the Grand Canal was here, and this is the oldest of the present four bridges, completed in 1591 to the design of Antonio da Ponte. Its stone arch rests on 6000 wooden piles at each side, and it was the first bridge to have the bedding joints of the stone blocks set perpendicular to the line of thrust of the arch, later a standard procedure. Rents from the colonnade of shops, not an integral structural feature, helped to defray maintenance costs.

Malmsmead Bridge, Oare, Somerset, England
Badgworthy Water here forms the boundary between Somerset and Devon, and the 17th-century humpback bridge stands alongside an ancient ford. With two round arches, it is a packhorse bridge, 2.9m (9.5ft) wide, built of coursed local rubblestone without any pretension to elegance, but with a natural harmony of appearance.

Stara Ćuprija (Old Bridge), Konjic, Bosnia-Herzegovina
Ali-aga Hasečić is commemorated as architect of this asymmetrical five-arched bridge over the Neretva River, built in 1682–83. The apex is above a pier rather than over an arch. Pointed cutwaters on the upstream side are balanced by rounded buttresses on the downstream face. The bridge was destroyed in March 1945 and rebuilding was completed in June 2009.

Yulong Bridge, Yangshuo, China
Yulong means 'dragon encounter' and a dragon legend is associated with the origin of the bridge, which was built around 1412, in the Yongle period of the Ming dynasty. Picturesquely overgrown with Chinese wisteria and vines, its soaring arch and stepped profile give it a strong character, appropriate to the remarkable scenic area in which it stands.

LEFT:
Shaharah Bridge, Yemen
At 2600m (8530ft) above
sea level, in the al-Ahnum
Mountains, a 17th-century
stone bridge supports the
paved track to the remote
village of Shaharah, over a
chasm 200m (656ft) deep.
Salah al-Yaman was the
constructor and the bridge
is 20m (65.6ft) long and 3m
(9.8ft) wide. Its deck is level,
but a set of steps climbs
upwards from the centre
point to continue the
dizzying pathway.

RIGHT:
**Ponte dei Sospiri (Bridge of
Sighs), Venice, Italy**
A corridor bridge, designed
by Antonio Contino and built
in 1600, it links the Doge's
Palace to the 'New Prison',
spanning the narrow Rio
del Palazzo. Built of white
limestone, with baroque
ornamentation including
mascaroons (carved faces)
on the voussoirs, it has long
borne its romantic nickname.

Si-o-se Pol (33-Arch Bridge), Isfahan, Iran
Completed in 1602, also known as Allahverdi Khan Bridge, after Shah Abbas's chancellor, it crosses the Zayandeh Rud River on 33 arches. The upper level arcade carries a paved way on top. With spaces for meeting and contemplation, the bridge was a key element in the Shah's grand plan for the city.

ABOVE:
Puente de Piedra (Stone Bridge), Zamora, Spain
Maintained in reconstructed form from 1712, its origins go
back to the late 12th century. Massive piers and 16 arches, with
relieving arches in the spandrels, help to cope with the Douro's
occasional floods, but repairs have been frequent in its history.
At some point it lost its stone parapets and is bordered by
metal railings.

LEFT:
Pont Neuf, Paris, France
Despite the 'new bridge' name, it is the oldest surviving bridge
over the Seine in Paris, inaugurated in 1607. It was also new
in its design concept, built to carry heavy loaded wagons, and
with the novelty of pedestrian pavements. No toll was charged,
and it became the city's most popular meeting place.

BELOW:

Arta Bridge, Arachthos River, Greece
Dating in its present form from the early 17th century, when Greece was part of the Ottoman Empire, the Arta Bridge is associated with a folk-tale of human sacrifice to assure its safety. There are four arches, and its profile is unusual, with the main span close to one bank.

RIGHT:

Somerset Lifting Bridge, Bermuda
Claimed as the world's smallest working drawbridge, it links Somerset Island to Bermuda, and was built in 1620. Its central deck, once raised by a hand crank, is now a retractable panel between two cantilevered wooden half-spans, allowing passage to yachts.

ABOVE:
Gongchen Bridge, Hangzhou, China
Its name meaning 'Emperor's meeting place', the bridge marks the end of the Grand Canal between Beijing and Hangzhou. Built in 1631 on marshy ground, resting on timber piles, it was rebuilt in 1712–17 after collapsing. The masonry courses of the arch are laid without mortar. Protective carved monsters on separate plinths flank the central piers.

RIGHT:
Korenbeursbrug (Cornmarket Bridge), Leiden, Netherlands
Set on raised abutments to allow boats to pass on a canalised arm of the Rhine, the bridge was built in 1642 and was the site of the city's corn market. The classical-style market building was added in 1825. Restored in 1978, the bridge is now part of a vibrant bankside street market.

LEFT:
Pol e-Khaju (Khaju Bridge), Isfahan, Iran
Built around 1650, this bridge forms a companion on the Zayandeh Rud to the Si-o-se Bridge, and is also on two levels with an upper arcade topped by a walkway. Unlike the older bridge, it also functions as a weir, with sluices beneath the 23 arches. Traces of original wall paintings and tiling can still be seen.

ABOVE:
Watendlath Bridge, Cumbria, England
A typical Lake District pack-horse bridge, probably built during the 18th century, using a mixture of locally available slate and rubble stone. The narrow voussoirs are slate. It was seriously weakened in severe flooding in December 2015 and a restoration prgramme is planned.

OVERLEAF:
Kintai Bridge, Iwakuni, Japan
Its five arches, seeming to float up from their solid stone piers, present a superb example of all-wood construction, using Japanese zelkova, pine, cypress, chestnut and oak. In this form the bridge dates back to 1673, though rebuilding was required in 1950 when the arches were washed away. *Kintai* means 'gold brocade sash'.

LEFT:

Gamle Bybro (Old Town Bridge), Trondheim, Norway
Built between 1681 and 1685 over the Nidelva River, of wood in truss form on three stone pillars, and with a bascule lifting span to allow small ships to pass, it was reconstructed in 1861 and again in 1950 when the bascules were removed. The preserved chain supports are known as '*Lykkens portal*', Gate of Happiness.

ABOVE:

Barrage Vauban, Strasbourg, France
The great military engineer Sebastien Vauban designed this structure, finished in 1690 and acting as bridge, defence work and dam on the River Ill (replacing the Ponts Couverts). Barriers could be dropped to block the river and flood the surrounding area. The higher arches permitted boats to pass, with drawbridges on the inside passageway.

RIGHT:

Aqueduct of Vauban, Château de Maintenon, France
The remains of an aqueduct begun in 1686 but never completed, crossing the Eure River, part of an 80km (50 mile) system to carry water to the gardens of Versailles. Cutting right across the park of the Château de Maintenon, originally planned as a triple arcade resembling the Pont du Gard, with a height of 74m (243ft), its ruins are 28.5m (94ft) high.

18th & 19th Century Bridges

Most bridges in the eighteenth century were still built of natural materials, stone and wood, although the use of bricks in larger bridges was becoming more frequent. The scientific approach to bridge design, already begun in the 16th century, was further developed, resulting in bridges of greater span, and with narrower piers, and so using less material and saving costs: Paris's Pont de la Concorde is a prime example. This was also the century in which steam power was established and before its end, bridges made entirely of iron had been introduced. The new science of metallurgy helped to speed up development and iron bridges became increasingly common once designers understood the capacity of cast iron for bearing tension, and of wrought iron for compression. Indeed, the 19th century saw the construction of more bridges than in all the previous centuries put together. This was due to the extremely rapid spread of railways, with the 'iron road' very often using iron bridges to pass over or under obstacles. At the same time, improved road construction led to the building and rebuilding of many bridges. Later in the century, steel was increasingly favoured for its lightness, strength and durability, a process which reached its climax in the massive cantilevered towers of the Forth Bridge. By then, too, reinforced concrete was just beginning to be used.

LEFT:
Puente Nuevo (New Bridge), Ronda, Spain
Bridges could be used for other purposes apart from the obvious one. The Puente Nuevo at Ronda, Spain (1793), looking almost like the facade of a building, has an enclosed space beneath the roadway, sometimes used as a prison, now a visitor centre.

ABOVE AND LEFT:

Holzbrücke (Wooden Bridge), Bad Säckingen, Germany
On the Upper Rhine, with one end in Germany and the other in Switzerland, it is Europe's longest roofed bridge, at 203.7m (668ft). The present form, on stone piers, goes back to a rebuild in the 1690s, though floods and fires have required further repair work, and hydro-electric works made a rebuild necessary in the 1960s.

RIGHT:

Luding Chain Bridge, China
An exciting way to cross the Dadu River since 1710, the Chain Bridge is also a landmark in modern Chinese history as the scene of an early victory by the Communist Red Army in 1935. Suspended on 13 chains, of which nine form the floor, with wooden planking, and two provide handrails, its span is 103m (338ft) and it is 2.8m (9.2ft) wide.

LEFT:

The 'Seventeen Hole' Bridge, Beijing, China

From the east bank of Kunming Lake, in the Summer Palace Complex, its name referring to its 17 arches, it reaches to the South Lake Island in an elongated humpback form. Dating to the reign of Emperor Qianlong, pre-1799, it is adorned with 544 carved lions and some larger sculptures including a bronze buffalo, intended to keep floods at bay.

RIGHT:

Arcos da Lapa, Rio de Janeiro, Brazil

Also known as the Carioca Aqueduct, inaugurated in 1750, though begun in 1723 as part of a water supply system for the city, its 42 two-storey arches, in austere military style, stretched for 270m (886ft), at a height of 17.6m (57.7ft). By the 1890s it was redundant, but found a new role as conduit for the Santa Teresa tramline, which it still provides.

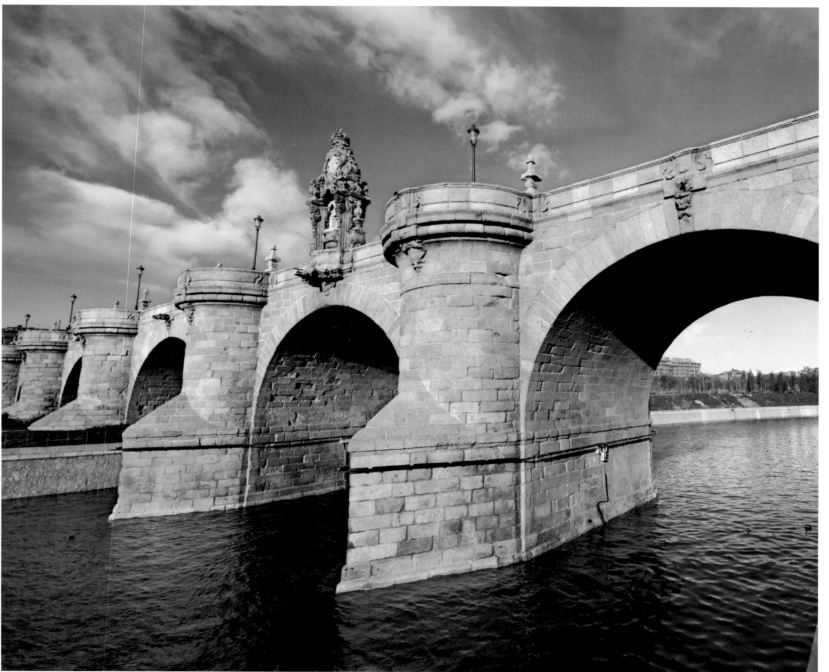

LEFT:

Puente de Toledo, Madrid, Spain

The architect Pedro da Ribera designed this nine-span baroque bridge over the Manzanares River, built between 1718 and 1732. Of granite masonry, it shows no structural advance over the earlier Segovia Bridge. Statues of Saint Isidore and his wife Saint Maria Torribia are mounted on the sides. In 1972–74 it was restructured as a pedestrian footbridge.

RIGHT:

Lejonströmsbron (Lejonström Bridge), Skellefteå, Sweden

Sweden's oldest surviving wooden bridge was built over the Skellefte River in 1737, its deck mounted on short wooden trestles on top of stone piers, and supported by lateral braces. Its six spans, 207.5m (680.7ft) long and 5m (16.4ft) wide, have to withstand winter ice as well as summer sun. It was the site of a battle in the Finnish War of 1809.

ABOVE:

Venedictos Bridge, Grevena Prefecture, Greece
On a spectacular site where the Venetikos River emerges from
the Portitsa Gorge, the bridge was built in 1743 to improve
communication between villages and monasteries in the region.
Its inverted v-shape profile and pointed arch are typically
Ottoman. The span is 34m (111.5ft), width 2.7m (8.86ft), and
height 7.8m (25.6ft).

RIGHT:

Jade Belt Bridge, Beijing, China
Spanning the outlet from Kunming Lake to the Yu River in the
Summer Palace Complex, the high arch was designed to allow
passage to the imperial barge. But it is also known as 'Moon
Bridge': the arch and its reflection in the water making a full
circle. Built between 1715 and 1764, its name comes from the
decorated archivolts, said to resemble jade ornaments.

Pulteney Bridge, Bath, England
In Palladian style, by the architect Robert Adam, with limestone masonry, its three equal arches have spanned the River Avon since 1774. The buildings, intended as shops, were integral to the general design. Numerous alterations in later years have not spoiled its charm.

LEFT:
Figured Bridge, Tsaritsyno Park, Moscow, Russia
Designed by V.I. Bazhenov for Empress Catherine the Great, in almost-Gothic style, and built between 1776 and 1778, it was part of a grandiose project for a palace and park. Of patterned bricks and white stone, with semicircular turrets, it was situated so as to conceal, then reveal the palace beyond.

ABOVE:
Siberian Marble Gallery, Tsarskoe Selo, Russia
Set in another imperial domain, this 1774 bridge, spanning a rivulet, was based on an English model, at Wilton House. The use of blue-grey and white marble from the Ural Mountains gave it the 'Siberian' name. The base is granite. Like the previous example, it shows a bridge intended purely as a landscape feature.

RIGHT:
The Iron Bridge, Ironbridge, England
The shape of things to come was shown in 1779 by the world's first bridge made of iron. Designed by Thomas Pritchard and built by Abraham Darby, its five main ribs and supports are made from 378 tons of cast iron from Darby's foundry. Its apex is 15.8m (52ft) above the River Severn and its width of 5.5m (18ft) was intended to allow two-way traffic.

ABOVE:
Lomonosov Bridge, St Petersburg, Russia
Known until 1948 as the Chernyshev Bridge, it was built in the late 18th century as a lifting bridge over the Fontanka River. Until 1913 the lifting span was of wood, replaced then by a steel plate. The pavilions housed the raising mechanism, which is no longer in use, though the hoisting chains remain in place.

RIGHT:
Alte Brücke (Old Bridge), Heidelberg, Germany
Properly known as the Karl Theodor Bridge, built 1786–88, its seven sandstone arches cross the River Neckar. The medieval gate of an earlier bridge still stands at the city end. Statues of Prince Karl Theodor and of Minerva decorate it, though its real symbol is the little statue of a monkey. Blown up in 1945, it was rebuilt in 1946–47.

LEFT:

Pont de la Concorde, Paris, France

A significant part of Paris's late 18th-century cityscape, the bridge was built between 1787 and 1791, as the final work of the great designer Jean-Rodolphe Perronet. Its elegant form embodies his theories and practice in the relation of piers to arches. Its width was doubled in 1930–32 but its classic lines were preserved.

RIGHT:

Halfpenny Bridge, Lechlade, England

Opened in 1792, this former toll bridge (hence the name) marks the head of navigability on the Thames. Built of Cotswold stone, its width is only 6m (19.7ft) and traffic is controlled by lights. Two smaller, unequal arches are set in the south abutment.

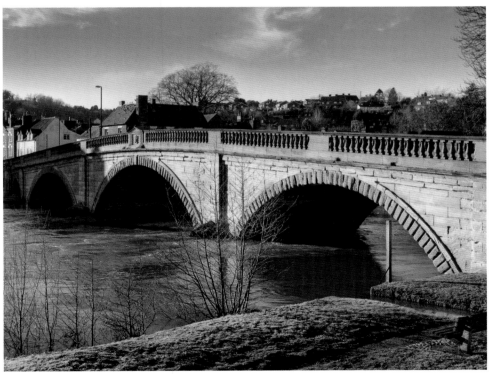

LEFT:

Old Bridge, Bewdley, England

Floods on the River Severn have destroyed many bridges, but this one has stood since 1798. Designed by Thomas Telford, it has a gentle humpback profile over three main arches, the central one of 18m (59ft) span.

ABOVE:

Norrbro (North Bridge), Stockholm, Sweden

Stockholm's first stone bridge, it forms part of the neoclassic scheme devised for the city centre in the late 18th century. Crossing the Norrström (North River) via the Helgeandsholmen island, it has one arch on the north side, completed in 1787, and three on the south, completed in 1806.

OPPOSITE:

Puente Nuevo (New Bridge), Ronda, Spain

The Guadalevin River cuts a 120m (394ft) deep gorge through Ronda and at 98m (321.5ft) this is the highest bridge to cross it. Built between 1759 and 1793, with massive piers and retaining walls, its total span is 66m (216.5ft).

ABOVE:

Pontcysyllte Aqueduct, Llangollen, Wales
Cast iron arches and waterway set on high stone pillars, at a maximum height of 38m (124.7ft) above the River Dee, make the traverse of Thomas Telford's canal aqueduct, completed in 1805, an exciting experience. Its length is 307m (1007ft) and its width, including towpath, is 3.4m (11.2ft).

RIGHT:

Ha'penny Bridge, Dublin, Ireland
Built in 1815 for pedestrians, this is an early iron bridge, still largely formed of the original Shropshire cast iron, which was shipped over in 18 separate pieces. It crosses the River Liffey in a single span of 43m (141ft). A renovation was carried out in 2001.

Sligachan Old Bridge, Isle of Skye, Scotland
The Cuillin Hills make a dramatic background to this bridge over the Sligachan River, built by Thomas Telford around 1815 as part of a road improvement scheme, of local rubblestone, in the simple, solid style of his smaller bridges.

LEFT:

Conwy Suspension Bridge, Conwy, Wales
Another design by the ubiquitous (in Great Britain) Thomas Telford. Built between 1822 and 1826, its machicolations were intended to harmonize with the adjacent medieval castle. Wrought iron chains supporting its 99.7m (327ft) span were reinforced by wire cables in 1903.

ABOVE:

Pont de Pierre (Stone Bridge), Bordeaux, France
Commissioned by Napoleon Bonaparte, its 17 arches match the number of letters in his name. It is the city's oldest bridge over the Garonne River, completed in 1822. Now it is primarily used by trams, pedestrians and cyclists.

RIGHT:

Kilenclyukú Híd (Nine-Hole Bridge), Hortobágy National Park, Hungary
On the main route from Budapest to the east, claimed as Hungary's longest stone bridge at 167.3m (549ft), its nine arches of whitewashed stone and brick stand out in the flat landscape. Completed in 1833, its fame inspired an annual fair which is still held.

LEFT:

Széchenyi Bridge, Budapest, Hungary

Best known as the Chain Bridge, it was the first permanent bridge across the Danube between Buda and Pest, designed by an English engineer, William Tierney Clark, and opened in 1849. The chains, massive iron links, are suspended between two arched stone towers. Destroyed in January 1945, it was reconstructed in 1949.

RIGHT:

Royal Border Bridge, Berwick, England

Completing the London-Edinburgh railway, Robert Stephenson's 28-arch viaduct was opened by Queen Victoria in 1850. Stone-built, except for brick under-arches, it spans the valley of the River Tweed for 659m (2162ft) at a maximum height of 37m (121ft).

ABOVE:
Bridge of Sighs, Cambridge, England
Named after the Venetian bridge, though not a copy, this
Victorian Gothic corridor bridge was built over the River Cam
in 1831 to link two parts of St John's College in Cambridge
University.

LEFT:
U Bein Bridge, Amarapura, Myanmar
Between 1849 and 1851 this teakwood bridge was built across
the Taung Tha Man Lake, using timbers from a dismantled
palace. In total 1086 pillars support it, some of the originals now
replaced by concrete. It is 1209m (3967ft) long, with four wooden
pavilions, and nine movable spans to allow boats to pass.

RIGHT:
'Bridge of Lies', Sibiu, Romania
Claimed as the oldest cast-iron bridge in Romania, built in
ornamental style in 1859, it crosses above an entrance road in the
hilly town of Sibiu, replacing a wooden structure. The nickname
long predates it and several legends exist as to how it arose.

Konitsa Bridge, Greece
Between the high banks of
the Aoos River, this bridge
was built by local initiative in
1870–71 and rises to an apex
of 20m (65.7ft) above the
water. A bell mounted below
the arch is activated by strong
winds to warn travellers: the
parapet walls are very low.

LEFT:
Huc Bridge, Hanoi, Vietnam
Part of a Buddhist religious complex in the Old Quarter of Hanoi, this red-painted wooden footbridge was built in the mid-19th century to give access to Ngoc Son Temple on Jade Island, set in Hoan Kiem Lake. Its name means 'absorbing the beautiful light'.

ABOVE:
Clifton Suspension Bridge, Bristol, England
Designed by Isambard Kingdom Brunel, but not built until after his death, opening in 1864. It follows Brunel's design in a somewhat modified form. Between two 'Egyptian' towers, six independently mounted wrought iron chains hold up the bridge deck, 101m (331ft) above the Avon Gorge.

RIGHT:
Rakotzbrücke, Park Kromlau, Germany
The bridge as landscape feature: built in an ornamental park around 1860, this semicircular 'ruined' arch of basalt blocks makes a perfect circle with its own reflection in the Rakotz lake. To help generate atmosphere, it was given the name of *Teufelsbrücke*, 'Devil's Bridge'.

OVERLEAF:
Kuldiga Bridge, Latvia
The Venta River has been spanned at Kuldiga since 1874 by this 164m (538ft) bridge. Its seven arches are of red clay brick, mounted on stone piers. Since restoration in 2005 it has become a focus for light shows and other displays.

LEFT:

Margit Híd (Margaret Bridge), Budapest, Hungary
The French architect Ernest Gouin designed Budapest's second Danube bridge, crossing close to Margaret Island and angled to face both river channels directly. Completed in 1876, its seven spans are formed of arched steel trusses, and sculptures decorate the stone piers. Destroyed in World War II, it was rebuilt, and renovated in 2009–11.

ABOVE:

Brooklyn Bridge, New York, USA
Finished in 1883 after 14 years building, it was the first steel wire suspension bridge, spanning the East River 84.3m (276.5ft) above high water, its neo-Gothic towers making a city landmark. Concerns about the wire quality led to the addition of stayed cables, so that technically it is a hybrid structure.

LEFT:

Capilano Suspension Bridge, Vancouver, Canada
Slung across the Capilano River in 1889, it is 80m (262ft) high and 140m (459ft) long. Originally a rope bridge, it was fitted with wire cables in 1903 and completely remade in 1956. Since 2011 it has been part of a cliffwalk route.

ABOVE:

Flume Covered Bridge, New Hampshire, USA
Located in this lumbering district since 1871, though possibly moved from a previous site, and crossing the Pemigewasset River, it is built on the truss system devised by Peter Paddleford. A pedestrian walkway is attached. The original roof of wooden planks was replaced by shingles in 1951.

RIGHT:

Forth Railway Bridge, Scotland
The great double cantilever towers of this bridge have carried the railway over the Firth of Forth since 1890, and are the classic example of 19th-century steel engineering. The bridge is 2.53km (1.57 miles) long, the rails are 48m (157.4ft) above the water, and the towers are 110m (361ft) high. It was last refurbished in 2011.

LEFT:

Lispole Viaduct, Kerry, Ireland

Five arches of rubblestone and brick, and two cast iron trusses carried the 91cm (3ft) gauge Tralee & Dingle Railway across the Owenalondrig River on a falling grade from right to left, levelling at the central span. Built in 1891, the line has been wholly disused since 1953.

RIGHT:

Tower Bridge, London, England

A very modern bridge for 1894, despite its Gothic-style architecture. It combines suspension cables for the side spans, hydraulically-powered bascules for the lifting section, and a high-level latticed steel covered walkway. Initially unpopular, it is now a major tourist attraction.

20th Century Bridges

Bridge engineering and architecture showed a relish for challenge in the 20th century, with an appetite for new techniques of design and new materials in construction. Reinforced concrete and steel largely replaced stone and wood except for small bridges. Suspension bridges had spans of a length previously thought impossible, and cable-stayed bridges became much more common. Very rarely, things went terribly wrong, as with the failure of the Tacoma Narrows suspension bridge in the USA, in 1940. Warfare caused the destruction of many historic bridges, often rebuilt in their previous form. New bridges became ever longer and higher, spanning stretches of sea and even linking continents, like the First Bosphorus Bridge in 1973. Planning, design and logistics became more vital as projects became more ambitious and expensive, and had to be viewed as a whole rather than a series of parts. The advent of computers helped enormously, bringing not only speed but a new flexibility to bridge design. Techniques changed. Riveting and welding, rather than using bolts, became the norm in metal bridges. The use of expansion joints was supplanted by jointless structures set on flexible bearings. Greater understanding of soil and rock formation and movement resulted in bridges more resistant to earth tremors. Bridge decks became lighter, but also stronger. Late in the century, in parallel with developments in building design, bridge designers often sought a distinctive appearance which was conditioned not only by function, as in the 19th century, but by a deliberate intention to show off the capacities of the materials, and the creativity of the designers. Great bridges have always been prestige symbols: in that respect at at least, nothing has changed.

LEFT:
Tower Bridge, Old Sacramento, California, USA
Opened in December 1935, this is a lifting bridge over the Sacramento River. Its towers are concrete sheathed in steel, and contain sliding weights to counterbalance the weight of the 64m (210ft) long central span in raising and lowering. Until 1963 it carried two roadways separated by a railroad track; since then it is a four-lane roadway. The gold paintwork was applied in 2002.

Mexican Canyon Trestle, New Mexico, USA
The Alamagordo & Sacramento Mountain Railroad built this wooden trestle bridge in 1899–1900 to give access to lumber country. With a length of 98m (321.5ft), it rises 16m (52.5ft) above the canyon floor, without railings or a refuge for lineside workers. The structure still stands, though the rails have been lifted and the end-timbers removed, in what is a popular walking and cycling area.

Victoria Falls Bridge, Zambia

Envisioned as part of a Cape-to-Cairo Railway, this parabolic-arch steel bridge was constructed in England and shipped in parts for assembly at its scenic location by the Second Cataract of the Falls. Opened in 1905, it is 198m (650ft) long and 128m (420ft) above the Zambesi River, carrying a road, the Zambia-Zimbabwe railway, and a footpath.

LEFT:

Solkan Bridge, Nova Gorica, Slovenia
Built in 1904–05, this bridge is claimed as the world's largest
stone-built arch, with a span of 85m (279ft) over the Soča River,
carrying the Jesenice-Goriča railway. In 1916, it was destroyed,
and rebuilt in 1925–27 with four arches in the spandrels rather
than the original five. Its total length is 219.7m (721ft).

ABOVE:

Glienicker Brücke, Potsdam, Germany
The Glienicke Bridge across the Havel River, linking Berlin
and Potsdam, opened in 1907, is a steel truss design intended
to bear the weight of heavy traffic. Damaged in 1945, it was
repaired by 1949 and formed part of the border between East
and West Germany (and a site for some notorious spy swaps)
until the unification of 1990.

LEFT:

Yutengping Bridge, Taiwan
Though ancient-looking, these are the remaining brick side-arches of a steel truss railway viaduct constructed by the Japanese in 1907 and destroyed by an earthquake in 1935. The line was diverted. The bricks were laid in European-style Flemish bond, though a local rice-based mortar was used. A further earthquake in 1999 toppled one of the surviving piers.

RIGHT:

Žvėrynas Bridge, Vilnius, Lithuania
When built in 1906 it was known as the Nikolay Bridge, joining Vilnius to the suburb of Žvėrynas over the Neris River. Its steel structure, resting on substantial stone piers, was manufactured in Warsaw, Poland, and assembled on site. The iron-work was renovated in 2006.

Pont de Cassagne, Pyrénées Orientales, France
Also known as the Gisclard Bridge after its designer, it is the only suspension bridge still in use on French railways. With a span of 156m (512ft) and a total length of 253m (830ft), its deck is 80m (262.4ft) above the Têt River, rising on a 60/1000 slope. The steel pylons, 30m (98.4ft) high, are set on masonry pillars.

LEFT AND BELOW LEFT:
Bolsheokhtinsky Most Bridge, St Petersburg, Russia
Formed of two bowstring trusses, with a central lifting span, electrically worked, to allow vessels on the Neva River to pass through, this bridge was opened in October 1911. Its ironwork was cast in Warsaw. The central pylons, of granite, are designed to resemble lighthouses. It was refurbished and the mechanism modernized in 1993–97.

RIGHT:
Manhattan Bridge, New York, USA
Overcrowding on the Brooklyn Bridge of 1883 spurred the building of this suspension bridge, which was opened in December 1909, to a design by Leon Moissieff, which anticipates the longer suspension bridges to come. With a width of 37m (121.3ft), it carries seven lanes of roadway and four rail tracks, in addition to pedestrian and cycle ways.

Wind and Rain Bridge, Chengyang, China
On the Nanjiang River, in the Guangxi Autonomous Region, the Dong people have built traditional pagoda-type bridges, known as 'wind and rain' or 'flower' bridges. Mounted on bluestone piers, constructed entirely of wood, with no nails, and decorated with paintings and carvings, this one dates from 1916.

LEFT:

Jacques Cartier Bridge, Montreal, Canada

First known as the Harbour Bridge, it was built between 1926 and 1930, using 33,000 tons of steel, and in total has 40 spans, although the great 334m (1096ft) span, with its latticed steel truss over the St Lawrence's eastern channel, heightened to 36.6m (120ft) in 1957–58, dominates. In 2017, an interactive decorative lighting system was fitted.

ABOVE:

Michigan Avenue Bridge, Chicago, USA

Since 2010 called the Du Sable Bridge, it is a double-bascule structure across the Chicago River, completed in 1920 in a Beaux-Arts style modelled on the Pont Alexandre III in Paris. Its deck has two levels, with a walkway beneath the road. A restoration project was carried out in 2009.

Nine Arches Bridge, Gotuwala, Sri Lanka
Sri Lanka's longest and highest railway viaduct, opened in 1921, 24m (78.7ft) high and 91.4m (300ft) long, is a curving nine-span construction of stone and brick, part of an unusual section of line that crosses over itself in a 360 degree loop to gain height in its route through mountain country.

ABOVE:

Harbour Bridge, Sydney, Australia

With New York's Hellgate Bridge as a model, this was the world's largest steel through-arch bridge on its opening in 1932, formed with 53,000 tonnes of steel and six million rivets. Its top is 134m (440ft) above the water. The road deck is suspended from the parabolic arch by tensioned rods. Since 1998 visitors have been able to climb the southern arc of the bridge.

RIGHT:

Golden Gate Bridge, San Francisco, USA

Testing new technology and design theories, since 1937 its 1280m (4200ft) span has crossed San Francisco Bay (total length is 2737.4m, 1.7 miles), at 67m (220ft) above high water level. For 27 years it was the world's longest suspension bridge, and remains one of the most elegant and best-proportioned of the many now existing.

ABOVE:
Royal Gorge Bridge, Colorado, USA
From 1929 to 2001 this was the world's highest bridge, it
was built as a tourist attraction, not a transport artery. The
wooden deck, suspended from 46m (151ft) steel pylons, is
291m (955ft) above the Arkansas River, and its total length is
384m (1260ft). It sustained some damage by fire in 2013, but
it was quickly repaired.

RIGHT:
George Washington Bridge, New York–New Jersey, USA
An all-steel, two-deck suspension bridge, with main cables
almost one metre (3.3ft) in diameter, it links Manhattan and
New Jersey across the Hudson River. It was opened in 1931,
and the lower deck was added in 1961–62 to cope with vastly
increased traffic: with 14 lanes, it is reckoned to be the world's
busiest major bridge.

TOP LEFT:

Lions Gate Bridge, Vancouver, Canada
Opened in 1938, named for two nearby mountains, it crosses Burrard Inlet at a height of 61m (200ft) to allow ships to pass below. The main span is 473m (1552ft) long, and total length including approaches is 1,823m (5981ft). In a major renewal operation, the main bridge deck was replaced in 2000–01.

BOTTOM LEFT:

Goodpasture Covered Bridge, Oregon, USA
Still used by motor vehicles, the one-lane bridge, built in 1938, crosses the McKenzie River. Its roof and walls cover a wooden Howe truss. In truss designs the forces of compression and tension are distributed among the members: here the diagonal beams slant away from the centre to absorb compression, and the verticals are tensioned.

ABOVE:

Tara Bridge, Djurdjevića, Montenegro
Mijat Trojanović designed this open-structure concrete viaduct above the Tara Gorge with four approach spans and a main arch 116m (380.6ft) long and around 170m (558ft) high. Built in 1937–40, it was destroyed by partisans in 1942 and rebuilt in 1946. It is a popular bungee-jump site.

Howrah Bridge, Kolkata, India
Replacing a pontoon bridge over the Hooghly River, and built between 1936 and 1943, it is a balanced cantilever bridge, with a 172m (564ft) central section between cantilever arms. The road deck is suspended by 39 sets of steel rods from the base girders of the main structure. In 1965, the bridge was formally renamed Rabindra Setu.

River Kwai Bridge, Kanchanaburi, Thailand
Built in 1942–43 on the notorious 'Death Railway' from Thailand to Burma, and preceded by a temporary wooden structure, its combination of arched and straight steel girder trusses was built over the Mae Klong River (renamed Kwae Yai in the 1960s). Put out of action by Allied bombs in 1945, it was reinstated in 1946.

Lake Pontchartrain Causeway, Louisiana, USA
Opened in 1956, the 'causeway' is a prestressed concrete viaduct 38.4km (23.86 miles): the longest continuous bridge over water. A parallel bridge was completed in 1956, with seven crossovers between the two. The road decks are set on 9000 concrete piles. A bascule lifting section eight miles from the north end permits shipping to pass.

Crescent City Connection, New Orleans, USA
The first of these two bridges over the Mississippi was opened in 1958, at the time the longest continuous truss bridge in the world, and the second, downstream, followed in 1988. Both have a 480m (1575ft) main span and overall length of 4.1km (2.54 miles).

Evergreen Point Floating Bridge, Washington State, USA

In April 2016 a new floating bridge replaced the original 1963 bridge linking Seattle and Bellevue. Resting on 77 massive concrete pontoons, its deck is six metres (20.2ft) above the water, rising to 21.3m (71.8ft) in the east navigational span. At 2349.5m (1.46 miles) it is the world's longest floating bridge.

LEFT:

Zeelandbrug (Zeeland Bridge), Zeeland, Netherlands

The longest bridge in the Netherlands, this 5.02km (3.12 mile) concrete structure links the Schouwen-Duiveland and Noord-Beveland islands in the eastern arm of the Scheldt estuary. Built between 1963 and 1965, it has a 40m (131ft) lifting span for shipping.

LEFT:

Severn Bridge, England-Wales

Opened in 1966, this was among the first of the UK's long suspension bridges, with a main span of 987.5m (3240ft) between 132m (433ft) towers of tubular steel. Wind resistance was a major concern and the triangular arrangement of the cables and aerofoil section of the orthotropic deck were innovative features.

San Mateo-Hayward Bridge, California, USA
Replacing a low-level bridge, completed in 1967, this curving bridge is California's longest, at seven miles (11.2km), formed of concrete trestle spans with steel box girders on the 41.1m (134.8ft) high-rise section. It is an orthotropic structure, whose steel-plate deck both bears the traffic load and contributes to the overall strength of the bridge.

OPPOSITE TOP:

Ölandsbron (Öland Bridge), Kalmar, Sweden
Since 1972 this 6km (3.7 mile) bridge has linked the island of Öland with the Swedish mainland. It stands on 155 reinforced concrete pillars, rising at the western end to give 36m (118ft) clearance, and was until 1998 Europe's longest bridge. It carries the island's water supply as well as a four-lane highway.

OPPOSITE BOTTOM:

First Bosphorus Bridge, Istanbul, Turkey
In the 5th century BCE, the Persian King Darius had a floating bridge here to enable his army to cross. The first bridge above the strait between Europe and Asia was built between 1970 and 1973. The end towers are of steel, and the hangers that support the box girder deck are unusually arranged in angled pairs, meeting at the cable join. In 2016 it acquired the official name of 'July 15th Martyrs' Bridge'.

ABOVE:

New River Gorge Bridge, West Virginia, USA
Among the world's highest bridges, and the fourth-longest steel arch bridge, it was completed in 1977, carrying Route 19 at a height of 267m (876ft) above the New River. Cor-ten steel was used, which has high strength, weathers without rusting, and does not require painting.

Krčki Most (Krk Bridge), Croatia

Two reinforced concrete spans, using the rocky St Mark islet as a centre, reach to the Adriatic island of Krk. Completed in 1980, its total length is 1430m (4692ft) and the longer span over the Tihi Channel, whose arch, unusually, springs from below water level, is 390m (1280ft).

Seto Ohashi (Seto Great Bridge), Japan

Not one but a series of six two-deck suspension or cable-stayed bridges, crossing five islands in the Inland Sea to link Honshu and Shikaku, 13.1km (8.1 miles) long, and carrying both road and railway, it was completed in 1988.

Sunshine Skyway Bridge, Tampa Bay, Florida, USA

Officially the Bob Graham Sunshine Skyway Bridge, built 1982–97, crossing Tampa Bay in a combination of steel and pre-stressed concrete construction, with a cable-stayed central span giving a clearance of 55m (180.4ft) for shipping. Its total length is 6.7km (4.14 miles).

Nanpu Bridge, Shanghai, China

When opened in 1991, it was the world's fourth largest cable-stayed bridge, with a span of 423m (1388ft) across the Huangpu River, and a total length of 8,346m (27,382ft) including the approach spirals. The H-shaped towers are of reinforced concrete and the bridge deck is formed from a steel-concrete composite developed in China.

ABOVE:
Puente Lusitania (Lusitania Bridge), Mérida, Spain
Replacing the Roman bridge over the Guadiana River, the structure is a horizontal box girder of pre-cast, post-tensioned concrete, supported from above by 23 pairs of steel rods fixed to a steel tied arch with a 189m (620ft) span. It opened in 1991.

RIGHT:
Ikema Ohashi (Ikema Great Bridge), Okinawa, Japan
The road link between Ikema and Miyako Islands was formed in 1992 by the 1592m (5223ft) bridge, a two-lane roadway with a concrete deck set on single concrete piers. It was built to encourage tourists.

Rainbow Bridge, Tokyo, Japan
Connecting the city with Odaiba Island in Tokyo Bay,
this two-deck suspension bridge was finished in 1993.
The main span is 570m (1870ft) but with the approaches
the entire bridge is 798m (2618ft) long. The name was
decided by a public vote, and a coloured lighting system
is mounted on the cables.

ABOVE:

Wildlife Overpass, Icefields Parkway, Banff National Park, Canada

A bridge built exclusively for use by wild animals, this is one of numerous overpasses on highways through the National Parks of the Rocky Mountains from the 1990s, constructed in an effort to provide the animals with safe access to their habitat on both sides of the road.

RIGHT:

Freeway Interchange, Los Angeles, California, USA

Interstate Routes 105 and 110 meet at the Judge Harry Pregerson Interchange, where ramps and crossings on four levels allow traffic to enter and leave from any direction. Computers helped in planning the concrete construction, over 40m (131ft) high, opened in 1994. It incorporates passage for light-rail trains and dedicated bus lanes.

Tsing Ma Bridge, Hong Kong, China
Lantau Island is linked to Hong Kong since 1997 by this two-deck suspension bridge, the largest in the world to carry both road and rail traffic. With a main span of 1377m (4518ft), it is made from 49,000 tonnes of structural steel, and 160,000km (100,000 miles) of wire are woven into the main cable strands.

Confederation Bridge, Prince Edward Island, Canada
The Trans-Canada Highway was extended to Prince Edward Island with the opening of this 12.9km (8 mile) bridge in 1997. Its spans are formed of post-tensioned concrete box girders, constructed on-site, and designed for a 100-year lifespan. Protection against surface and floating ice was a major issue in construction.

Storabæltsbroen (Great Belt Bridge), Denmark
Joining the Danish mainland to the island of Zealand, the bridge opened in 1998. The entire structure, known as the fixed link, comprises the suspension bridge, longest outside Asia at 1624m (5328ft) to the island of Sprogø, and a road/rail box girder bridge to Zealand.

LEFT:

Ponte Vasco da Gama, Lisbon, Portugal

Europe's longest bridge, crossing the Tagus estuary to bypass Lisbon. The cable-stayed main span is 420m (1378ft) and the full length is 12.34km (7.67 miles). It is built to withstand a major earthquake, and to have a life expectancy of 120 years.

RIGHT:

Chesapeake Bay Bridge-Tunnel, USA

A 36.8km (23 mile) fixed link across Chesapeake Bay, using a combination of concrete trestle bridge and undersea tunnel, it was opened to traffic in 1964, and hailed as a wonder of modern engineering. A second, parallel bridge section was completed in 1999. The northern trestle rests on 2,523 piles, the southern on 2,591.

**Akashi Kaikyo Ohashi
(Great Bridge), Kobe, Japan**
At 1991m (6270ft) long, in
2017 still the world's longest
suspension bridge. Linking
Kobe to Awaji Island, it
opened in 1998. Foundations
of the steel towers are sunk
in the sea-bed 60m (197ft)
below the surface, and they
rise 283m (928.4ft) above it.
The 1995 Kobe earthquake
did the unfinished bridge no
damage, but left it almost a
metre longer.

21st Century Bridges

Bridge design in the 21st century has been marked by a new freedom taken by designers, partly due to continuing development of new constructional materials and techniques that allow for adaptations of shape, giving a sculptured appearance that seems to transgress the old laws and guidelines. These materials, usually composites, can often be produced to order, in different colours. Another important factor, already apparent in the last two decades of the 20th century, is the ambition of engineers and architects to go one better than their predecessors in creating stylish and exciting structures that are also functional. In this they have been helped and encouraged by the rivalry between countries and cities to display an appearance of modernity (indeed, post-modernity). Much of the most advanced work has been done in great conurbations, where concentration of millions of people has put heavy strain on transport routes and systems. The three great bridges across the Bosphorus, with a fourth over the Hellespont to come, are evidence of the role bridges can play in such locations. The other notable scene of ultra-modern bridge design is in recreational areas, once favoured for ornamental bridges, but now often provided with such state-of-the-art structures as the Charles Kuonen Bridge, designed to thrill and amaze rather than to offer the kind of aesthetic spectacle provided by the park bridges of the imperial era. Ancillary aspects, like lighting, are increasingly employed. A great bridge at night, previously invisible apart from its tower warning lights, can now be a striking and flamboyant sight on a grand scale.

LEFT:
Øresund Bridge, Denmark-Sweden
A double-decked bridge, with Euroroute E20 above the railway, inaugurated on 1 July 2000, it connects Copenhagen in Denmark with Malmö in Sweden across the Øresund seaway, stretching 7.84km (4.9 miles) to the artificial island of Peterholm where it gives way to a tunnel. The cable-stayed main span is 490m (1608ft) with a sea clearance of 57m (187ft).

Millennium Bridge, London, England

Described as a 'blade of light' design, this is an unusual suspension bridge, with low-level cables borne on arms suspended from two piers set in the River Thames. Opened in 2000, it was closed almost immediately due to a problem with synchronous lateral excitation – a sideways sway caused by walkers – and reopened in 2002.

ABOVE:

Tsunoshima Ohashi (Tsunoshima Great Bridge), Shimonoseki, Japan

Bending round an islet in the Sea of Japan to reach Tsunoshima Island, this concrete bridge, 1780m (5840 ft) long, opened in 2000, was until 2015 the longest island-link bridge in Japan, and remains the longest that is also toll-free. Designed to be low-level, apart from the seaway section, unlike most bridges it goes downwards from the city end.

RIGHT:

Puente de la Mujer (Bridge of the Woman), Buenos Aires, Argentina

Opened in 2001, it is a swing bridge, designed by Santiago Calatrava. The entire central span, supported by cables from an inclined pylon 38m (125ft) high, rotates 90 degrees to open the waterway. Construction is of reinforced concrete and steel, faced with natural stone or ceramics at walking level.

ABOVE:
Goodwill Bridge, Brisbane, Australia
A pedestrians' and cyclists' bridge over the Brisbane River, opened in 2001. The main span is a 102m (335ft) steel arch, whose central end rests on a viewing platform known as the 'pavilion'.

RIGHT:
Shuibai Bridge, Guizhou Province, China
From its opening in 2001 until 2016, this was the world's highest railway bridge, crossing the Beipan River gorge at a height of 275m (902ft). Each half of the arch was built parallel to the valley and they were then rotated on special bearings to join each other, a technique developed by Chinese engineers.

LEFT:

Al Salam Peace Bridge, El Qantara, Egypt
Largely Japanese-funded, and Japanese-designed and built, it is a cable-stayed bridge over the Suez Canal, opened in 2001. Its towers, each a single bracing arch, are in the form of obelisks. The main span is 70m (230ft) above the canal and the gradually rising approach structures give a total length of 3.9km (2.4 miles).

RIGHT:

Hoge Brug (High Bridge) Amsterdam, Netherlands
Undulant and bright red, this footbridge arcs across a canal in Amsterdam's eastern docklands in two unequal spans. Its shape and netlike latticed steel pattern quickly gained it the nickname of 'Python Bridge' when it opened in 2001. In 2002 it won the International Footbridge Award.

Ponte Juscelino Kubitschek, Brasilia, Brazil

Inaugurated in 2002, crossing Lago Paranoá, designed by Alexandre Chan and Mario Vila Verde, the structure is simple yet startling. The roadway is suspended from steel arches placed in skew formation, and propped by sloping concrete supports. The total length is 1200m (3937ft).

Dongting Lake Bridge, Hunan Province, China
Crossing the lake where it meets the Yangtze River, three fork-shaped central towers of pre-stressed concrete support the cable-stayed section of this 10.17km (6.32 mile) bridge, which opened to traffic in 2001. MR (magnetorheological) dampers were applied in 2002 to suppress wind-induced vibration in the 156 longest cables.

Rama VIII Bridge, Bangkok, Thailand
As often with cable-stayed bridges, it is asymmetrical in form. A single inverted-Y pylon, 160m (525ft) high near the west bank supports a double row of cables on the main span and a single row on the approach span. Crossing the Chao Phraya River, it was opened in 2002.

Jambatan Seri Wawasan, Putrajaya, Malaysia
In Malaysia's new capital, this bridge, opened in 2003, spans the artificial Putrajaya Lake. A cable-stayed design, it has a single forward-leaning pylon supported by two curved backstays reaching almost to its 96m (315ft) top. The somewhat sail-like effect is enhanced by the pattern of the cables, especially in night-time illumination.

LEFT:

Bolshoy Obukhovsky Most (Big Obukhovsky Bridge), St Petersburg, Russia
Its first part completed in 2004, the twin span following in 2007, the cable-stayed double bridge, making the cross-Neva section of the city's ring road, clears the river with 30m (98.4ft) of height and gives the only night-time crossing.

ABOVE:

Lalon Shah Bridge, Paksey, Bangladesh
Opened in 2004, built downstream of the 1915 railway bridge over the Padma River, it is a segmental contruction of box girder sections on single pillars, using altogether 65,000 tonnes of concrete. Its length is 1800m (5906ft).

RIGHT:

Viaduc de Millau, France
The word's tallest bridge sweeps over the Tarn valley on a gentle curve near Millau, the tallest of its seven piers reaching to 343m (1,125.7ft). Designed by Foster & Partners of London in collaboration with French engineers, it has been described as 'environmental sculpture'. Opened in 2004, its design life is projected at 120 years.

LEFT:

BP Pedestrian Bridge, Chicago, USA
Completed in 2004 of stainless steel, reinforced concrete and hardwood (for the deck), the sinuous bridge links two parts of Chicago's Grant Park across busy Columbus Drive. Built to a design by Frank Gehry, the complex geometry of its sculptural style required 10,400 stainless steel trapezoidal panels in 17 different configurations.

RIGHT:

Sundial Bridge, Redding, California, USA
Solely for walkers' and cyclists' use, the bridge, designed by Santiago Calatrava, has the unique property of also being a sundial, its 66m (217ft) angled pylon fulfilling the function of the gnomon. Opened in 2004, it is a cable-stayed cantilever bridge, with stays on the span side only.

Sea Cliff Bridge, New South Wales, Australia
Opened in 2005, this is a shoreline, coast-hugging bridge 455.6m (1494.7ft) long, of balanced cantilever design and steel and reinforced concrete construction, providing a passage in an area where cliff falls made a wholly land-based road impracticable.

LEFT:
Donghai Bridge, Shanghai, China
The S2 Hulu Expressway takes to the sea for 32.5km (20.2 miles) to link Shanghai with Yangshan Port. Opened in 2005, the S-shaped bridge is mostly of segmental concrete spans on double-column piers, with a cable-stayed main and three auxiliary navigational spans. An associated wind farm of 34 turbine towers, 136m (446ft) high, is projected.

ABOVE:
Sky Bridge, Pulau Langkawi, Malaysia
Accessed by a cable car, this mountain-top bridge on Langkawi Island curves for 125m (410ft) around a single angled steel pylon and links two peaks. Opened in 2005, it is purely intended to offer visitors a spectacular experience. The walkway is formed of concrete (and some glass) panels, set on an inverted triangular steel truss.

ABOVE:

Svinesund Bridge, Norway–Sweden
Euroroute E6 is carried over the Iddefjord on the Norway–
Sweden border by a hollow reinforced concrete arch with a
steel box-girder deck on each side. Hangers from the arch
support transverse beams in the central section. It was opened
in 2005. Total length is 704m (2310ft), and it is 55m (180.4ft)
above the water.

RIGHT:

Bhumibol Bridges, Bangkok, Thailand
Between the two cable-stayed Bhumibol Bridges to the south
of Bangkok (opened in 2006) is a multi-level spiral interchange
above the Chao Phraya River, linking the north-south route over
the bridges with the western approach, and reaching a height
of 50m (164ft). Both built to the same design, the bridges have
concrete towers in elongated diamond shape.

Zhivopisny Most (Scenic Bridge), Moscow
Here is Europe's tallest cable-stayed bridge, hung from a steel arch rising 105m (344.5ft) above the Moskva River, which it crosses on a long diagonal. Opened in 2007, it carries a Metro line as well as a roadway. Weddings can be held in the pod at the top of the arch.

ABOVE:

Henderson Wave Bridge, Singapore
In parkland south of Singapore, this pedestrian bridge, 274m (899ft) long and up to 36m (118ft) above ground, has a wave-like structure based on the notion of a three-dimensionally folded surface, whose curving ribs undulate over and under the walkway. Set on concrete pillars, it is a construction of steel and wood, opened in 2008.

RIGHT:

Puente de l'Assut de l'Or, Valencia, Spain
In this harp-resembling design by Santiago Calatrava, opened in 2008, the 29 cable stays are secured to a curved pylon 118m (387ft) high with vertical backstays. The orthotropic steel deck has a span of 160m (525ft) and carries two three-lane roads, a tramline and pedestrian/cycle path.

LEFT:

Al Garhoud Bridge, Dubai, United Arab Emirates
Built between 2006 and 2008, and carrying 14 traffic lanes over Dubai Creek, built on asymmetrically splayed twin concrete piers, the bridge is 520m (1706ft) long and has a sophisticated decoration and colour scheme intended to resemble sand dunes by day and waves by night.

ABOVE:

Chaotianmen Bridge, Chongqing, China
With a main span of 552m (1811ft), this is currently the world's longest through-arch bridge, opened in 2009. Its two decks carry both road and metro railway over the Yangtse River in Chongqing. Steel in the structure weighs 45,000 tonnes. The approach spans are of concrete box girder type.

LEFT:

Tradeston Bridge, Glasgow, Scotland

Curvy geometry gives character to what locals call the 'Squiggly Bridge', opened in 2009, improving pedestrian and cycle access to the city centre. Its two concrete pylons are a variant on the cable-stayed approach, supporting a slender, slightly-arched S-shaped deck.

RIGHT:

Ponte Octávio Frias de Oliveira, São Paulo, Brazil

The potential of cable-stayed construction was pushed further here, with a single pylon supporting two curving bridge decks at different levels, opened in 2008. The X-shaped pylon is 138m (453ft) high and has 76m (249.3ft) of passage room. Like almost all such bridges, it has a complex illumination scheme built in.

LEFT:

Helix Bridge, Singapore

Linking Marina Centre with Marina South, this pedestrian bridge opened in 2010. The double-helix configuration of its stainless steel tubes and rods mirrors the structure of human DNA and is accentuated by the lighting scheme. Its length is 280m (919ft) and there are lateral viewing pods on the bay side.

ABOVE:

Jiaozhou Bay Bridge, Shandong Province, China

The world's longest sea bridge when it opened in 2011, with an aggregate length of 41.58km (26.4 miles), its construction required 450,000 tonnes of steel and 2.3 million cubic metres of concrete. It incorporates both suspension and cable-stayed sections, and has a multi-level over-sea interchange, with arms to Hongdao and Qingdao.

Tokyo Gate Bridge, Japan
Part of the Rinkai Tokyo
Port Seaway, opened in 2012,
it is a double-cantilever steel
truss structure, chosen to
provide adequate height
for shipping 54.6m (179ft)
without endangering aircraft
approaching Haneda Airport.
The shape of the pylons has
inspired the nickname of
'Dinosaur Bridge'.

LEFT:
Russky Bridge, Vladivostok, Russia
Currently the world's longest cable-stayed bridge, it was completed in 2012, crossing the strait from Vladivostok to Russky Island, with a main span of 1104m (3622ft), carrying a four-lane road. Its two towers, 320m (1050ft) high, rest on piles driven as much as 77m (253ft) into the ground.

RIGHT:
Zolotoy Rog Bridge, Vladivostok, Russia
Also opened in 2012, across Vladivostok's Zolotoy Rog (Golden Horn) inlet, and cable-stayed, its diverging pylons have a horn-like appearance. The main span is 737m (2417ft) and overall length is 1388m (4554ft).

Margaret Hunt Hill Bridge, Dallas, USA
On the west side of downtown Dallas, this cable-stayed bridge designed by Santiago Calatrava opened in 2012, spanning the Trinity River, its cables hanging from a 122m (400ft) high arch formed of welded steel tubes. The dynamic pattern of the cables reflects the curvature of the arch.

Pont Jacques Chaban-Delmas, Bordeaux, France
Europe's longest vertical-lift bridge, opened in 2013, allows large ships to pass on the Garonne River. Its 2600-tonne central lifting span is counterbalanced by 600-tonne weights in the four towers. The span is steel, the towers are concrete, with lighting systems that emphasise their vertical lines.

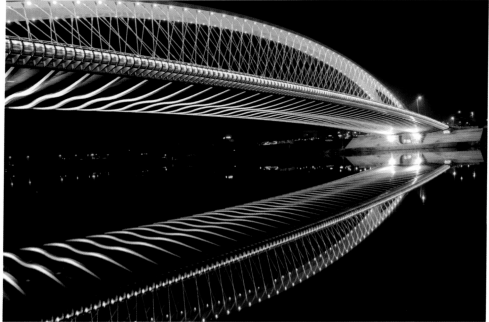

LEFT:
Trojsky Most (Troja Bridge), Prague, Czech Republic
A double-decked bowstring-arch bridge crossing the Vltava River, opened in 2014 and formed of both steel and concrete. The steel arch holds up the concrete deck through multiple hangers in a unique criss-cross design.

ABOVE:
Dragon Bridge, Da Nang, Vietnam
Completed in 2013, it crosses the Han River in two main arched steel spans, the longer being 200m (656ft) wide. With a smaller third arch, they are embellished with dragon-back spines, together with a decorative dragon's head capable of breathing out fire and water, to resemble a dragon leaping across.

RIGHT:
Duge Bridge, Guizhou Province, China
When completed in 2016 this was the world's highest bridge, its deck carrying the G56 expressway 565m (1,854ft) above the Beipan River. Cable-stayed, it has a main span of 720m (2363ft). In 2017, China had 17 of the world's 20 highest bridges.